The Night of R

Lailat-ul-Bara'h:

The 15th of Sha'ban

لَيْلَةُ الْبَرَاءَة

Dr Musharraf Hussain al-Azhari

بِسْمِ اللّٰهِ الرَّحْمٰنِ الرَّحِيمِ

Invitation Publications
Karimia Institute
512 Berridge Road West
Bobbersmill
Nottingham
NG7 5JU
England

Tel:+44 (0) 115 841 5806

email: info@karimia.com
http://karimia.com
http://introducingislam.co.uk

The Night of Repentance, Lailat ul Bara'h: The 15th of Sha'ban

Compiled and designed by Ghufran Shah, Series Editor, "Islamic Times, Places and People."

3rd Edition, July 2010

ISBN: 978-1-902248-50-9

Contents

Introduction

Allah ﷻ tells us in the Qur'an:

﴿ ... وَتُوبُوٓا۟ إِلَى ٱللَّهِ جَمِيعًا أَيُّهَ ٱلْمُؤْمِنُونَ لَعَلَّكُمْ تُفْلِحُونَ ﴾

"... And repent before Allah ﷻ together O believers so that you may prosper." (Surah an-Nur [24], ayah 31)

The Arabic noun, "*Taubah*" means to repent. Literally it means to return back, to turn back from evil to good, from sin to righteousness, from the displeasing to the pleasing, from hatred to love, and from God's disobedience to His obedience. Allah ﷻ tells us in the Qur'an:

﴿ وَمَن يَعْمَلْ سُوٓءًا أَوْ يَظْلِمْ نَفْسَهُۥ ثُمَّ يَسْتَغْفِرِ ٱللَّهَ يَجِدِ ٱللَّهَ غَفُورًا رَّحِيمًا ﴾

"And whoever does an evil or sins and then seeks forgiveness from Allah ﷻ, he will find Allah ﷻ All-Forgiving and All-Merciful." (Surah an-Nisa [4], ayah 110)

Repentance is necessary for two reasons:

Firstly, the burden of sins hardens the heart and this prevents one from worshipping Allah ﷻ and from doing good works. This is the curse of sin as one is deprived of Divine Mercy. Therefore to cleanse oneself from the filth of sin, it is necessary to repent so that one can taste the flavour of faith, worship and good works. To stay in a state of sin could eventually lead to *Kufr* (disbelief).

Secondly, a sin is Divine disobedience, thus the person has rebelled against his Lord and Sustainer. Therefore he owes Him an apology; he is indebted to his Lord. His good works will not be acceptable until he has paid his credit, i.e. until he has repented. Imam al-Ghazali رحمه الله says, "Do not put off repentance because you are too busy in worldly affairs. The world is only an illusion and deception. So call upon Allah ﷻ tearfully and in submission." (Minhaj ul-'Abidin)

The Night of Freedom (15th Sha'ban) لَيْلَةُ الْبَرَاءَة

The 15th night of the eighth lunar month of Sha'ban is called the "Night of Freedom", and there are several Ahadith that describe the nature of this wonderful night:

1. Mu'adh ﷺ says that the Messenger ﷺ said, "On the fifteenth night of Sha'ban, Allah ﷻ looks upon His creation with a special favour forgiving all except the idolater and the person full of rancour and hatred." (At-Tadhib wa at-Tarhib)
2. Aishah ﷺ reports that the Messenger ﷺ once asked me, "do you know what happens on the fifteenth of Sha'ban?" I replied no. He ﷺ then said on this night a list is prepared of all those that will be born and all those that will die that year. In this night, the people's works are raised to the heaven and their annual sustenance is fixed. (Mishkat)
3. Ali ﷺ used to say "On the night of the fifteenth of Sha'ban, do the night vigil and fast the next day. For Allah ﷻ manifests Himself on the sky from sunset announcing 'is there anyone out there seeking forgiveness so he could be forgiven? Is there anyone seeking sustenance so that he could be blessed with it? Is there anyone who is pain-stricken so that he could be relieved?' And so on and so on. This continues till the dawn. (Ibn Majah)
4. Aishah ﷺ says the Messenger ﷺ said Jibril ﷺ came to me and told me about the fifteenth of Sha'ban. "On this night Allah ﷻ frees people from hell in large numbers as large as the hair of Kalb's goats. However, He does not forgive the idolater, the one full of rancour, the one who breaks family ties, the one who is disobedient to his parents and the drunkard." (At-Tahdhib)

These are some of the Ahadith narrated by different companions about this night; it is a night of forgiveness and freedom from Divine wrath. How the Merciful Lord comes down to the sky offering His mercy and forgiveness to the earthly sinners. How should we spend this most wonderful night? The Messenger ﷺ, according to the hadith of Aishah رضي الله عنها did the following things during this night:

1. Visited the graveyard of Jannat-al-Baqi.
2. Prayed most of the night, spending a lot of time in prostration.
3. Made special Du‘a, "O Lord! You are forgiving, You love forgiveness, forgive us."

Imam Fakhr-ud-Din ar-Razi رحمه الله describes five distinct benefits of this great night:

1. Every important affair affecting human life is decided upon. Allah ﷻ says,
   ﴿ فِيهَا يُفْرَقُ كُلُّ أَمْرٍ حَكِيمٍ ﴾

   "In it [the Night of Power, or Ascension or Freedom] all matters of wisdom are differentiated." (Surah ad-Dukhan [44], ayah 4)

2. Excellence of worship. The Messenger ﷺ said whoever prays 100 rak‘ah of nafl, Allah ﷻ will send 100 Angels to bless him.
3. Showering of Divine Mercy. The Messenger ﷺ said Allah ﷻ forgives the sinners on this night and frees them from the chains of Hell.

Allah ﷻ forgives everyone, except the persistent and unsociable sinners like people full of anger, hatred of others, drunkards and those disobedient to parents.

The Messenger ﷺ interceded for his Ummah on the 13th of Sha'ban, he was granted one third. On the 14th of Sha'ban, he ﷺ was granted another third, and on the 15th of Sha'ban he ﷺ was granted the whole of his Ummah.

‘Ata’ ibn Yasar narrates: “On the 15th night of Sha‘ban the Angel of Death copies down the names of all those who will die from that Sha‘ban to the next Sha‘ban, and there is no night after *Laylat ul-Qadr* better than the 15th night of Sha‘ban.”

It is recommended to say the *du‘a:*

اللّهم إنّك عفوّ كريمٌ تحبّ العفو فاعْف عني، اللّهمّ إنّي أسْألك العفْو والعافية والمعافاة الدّائمة في الدّين والدّنيا والآخِرة

Allahumma innaka ‘Afūwun Karīmun tuhib ul ‘afwa fa‘afu ‘annī, Allahumma innī as’aluka al-‘afū, wa al-‘āfīyah wa al-mu‘āfāt ad-da’imah fī ad-dīni wa ad-dunyā wa al-ākhirah.

O Allah, You are Pardoning and Generous and You love to pardon, so pardon me. O Allah, I ask You for Your pardon, and constant well-being in this life, and in the hereafter.

What are the conditions of repentance?

Imam an-Nawawi ﷺ says there are three conditions of Taubah:

1. To give up the sin out of Divine fear.
2. To be ashamed and feel guilty of doing it.
3. To resolve not to repeat it again.

If the sin was against another person, then there is the fourth condition of requesting his/her pardon. If it involved taking someone’s wealth then it has to be returned or if it was a slander against someone then one must request forgiveness.

How can you give up sins?

Some people will say, ‘how can you give up sins when they are so tempting?’ Here one should recall the severe punishment of Allah ﷻ and the Lord’s displeasure. How can you withstand the hellfire? Will you be able to bear it? You cannot even bear the scorching sun, how will you then be able to bear roasting in the hellfire? Or the fire rods of hell angels? Or the venom of scorpions and snakes?

Finally, as an intelligent person how can you persist in sinning and committing crimes? Why do you like to be rebellious and mischievous? Why do you like to be unkind and inhumane to others? If you are mindful and conscious of these truths, then you will soon repent and turn back to the right path. If you have broken away from your Lord by not praying (the five daily prayers) or fasting or simply not carrying out His commandments then start doing these duties immediately and make up for the lost ones.

If you love something that is forbidden (like drinking alcohol, gambling or taking drugs), then give them up now.

If you have been unkind or unfair to someone (your parents, teachers, friends or relations) then ask for their forgiveness. Allah ﷻ will raise you in status. As the Prophets (peace be upon them all) said, "when you seek forgiveness from someone your status is raised."

The Prophet ﷺ used to seek Allah's ﷻ forgiveness and turn to Him in repentance more than seventy times every day! (Sahih al-Bukhari, narrated by Abu Hurairah ؓ) He ﷺ once described Allah's ﷻ pleasure at someone repenting as follows:

"Allah ﷻ is more pleased with the repentance of His slave than anyone of you is pleased with finding his camel which he had lost in the desert." (Sahih al-Bukhari, narrated by Anas ibn-Malik ؓ)

This is how pleased Allah ﷻ is when we repent and return to Him once more. SubhanAllah!

In another Hadith, the Prophet ﷺ said, "Allah ﷻ almighty extends His hand of forgiveness at night to forgive those who committed evil during the daytime and He extends his hand during the day to forgive those who committed evil during the night. He will do this until the sun rises from the west." (Muslim, narrated by Abu Musa al-Ash'ari ﵁)

For our moral development and spiritual enrichment, we must turn to our generous and loving Lord. The One Who created us, Who feeds us, protects us and cares for us and to Whom is our inevitable return.

Zikr: The Remembrance of God

The night of 15th Sha'ban is a blessed night, when the pious people immerse themselves in complete devotion and loving worship. Allah Says,

"..they spend the night for their lord prostrating, standing and crying O Lord! Turn away from us the punishment of the hell fire." (Surah al- Furqan [25], ayah 64)

They recite the Quran, do zikr and pray nafl all night. Zikr means remembrance, either with the heart alone or with the tongue alone, however, the best remembrance is that done by both and the remembrance with the heart alone is better than remembering with the tongue alone. Imam Nawawi has endorsed this view in his famous commentary of Muslim. He has also said that the remembrance of the heart is of two kinds: one is *taffakur* (also called Azikr-al Khafiy), which is contemplation.

The first kind of remembrance of the heart is the reflection in the creation of Allah ﷻ, this can be the study of nature and the environment or the whole universe. This reflection leads to and fear of Allah ﷻ as the majestic Lord and the creator; this deepens the belief in Tawhid. This is described in a hadith, "The best remembrance is reflection."

The second kind of remembrance of the heart is whenever one does something, he should remember Allah ﷻ, such that the fear of the Lord prevents him from doing the prohibited and the heart becomes free to remember Him, the Almighty. Remembrance is the opposite of forgetfulness, which is a state of mind. Hence, remembrance is the combined act of mind and the tongue, Allah ﷻ says:

"And remember your Lord whenever you forget Him" (Surah al- Kahf [18], ayah 24)

The Sufi Masters also stress the impact of remembrance of the heart and the excellence. According to them remembrance is to negate everything other than Allah ﷻ. In other words, the love of Allah ﷻ and Tawhid should replace the love of all other things. This is the whole purpose of remembrance.

There are four ways of remembering Allah ﷻ:

1. Remembrance only with the tongue whilst the heart is forgetful. This is a poor way of remembrance, but it still has value and effect.
2. Both the tongue and the heart are engaged. However, it is not fully established in the heart and requires a lot of effort.
3. The heart is fully engaged in the remembrance, such that it is not distracted. This is a wonderful state.
4. The thoughts of Allah ﷻ are dominant to such an extent that one cannot distinguish between the remembrance and the remembered. His heart is full of love of the lord and he drowns in it and becomes oblivious of the remembrance but engrossed in the remembered. The world in his sight appears as a poison, to be avoided at any cost. This is the state of *Fana* (annihilation and) this is the real remembrance.

The Significance of Du'a

The glorious Quran uses the word Du'a for a variety of meanings: devotion, seeking help, asking for something, word, call and praise (Muhammad ibn `Ulan in commentary on Riyadh-u-Saliheen).

Imam Fakhradeen Razi ﷺ defines Du'a as "The pleading of the servant to the Almighty Majestic Lord for his support, help and provision" (Tafseer Al-Kabeer).

In a spiritual context, Du'a refers to that sincere call, the earnest appeal and humble request, which the worshipper makes to his Almighty and Majestic Lord. This 'call' and sincere plea could be for help at a time of difficulty or for divine benevolence to shower mercy or merely for consolation and peace of mind. This gives the devout a sense of self-assurance, boosts self-confidence and makes one feel secure. What priceless gems in our turbulent time. Is it any wonder then why the Messenger ﷺ said, "Du'a is the essence of worship.

One of the Divine names is "Al-Mujeeb" the one who answers and replies to the call of his servants, *"call Me and I will answer you. (Surah Ghafir, ayah 60)"* says the Lord. Du'a is not only a form of the Lord's remembrance but also a pleasant experience. It generates spiritual energy that comforts the soul and is the coolness of the eye and gives peace of mind. Perhaps this is why the Messenger ﷺ likened the person who remembers Allah ﷻ to a living person; full of energy and vitality. On the other hand he likened the forgetful to a dead person.

A central verse on the topic of Du'a is the following:

"When my servants ask you about me, surely I am near, I answer the caller when he calls me so let them obey me and believe in me so they may be guided" (Surah al-Baqarah [2], ayah 186)

This verse raises some interesting questions, what were the circumstances of its revelation? What is the meaning of God's nearness? What is the point of making Du'a? Shouldn't we be satisfied with Divine decree anyway?

The caller pleads but his wish is never fulfilled – does the Du'a go unanswered?

Imam Razi ﷺ gives a masterly rebuttal to the challenge that these questions raise. He begins by mentioning the circumstance under which the ayah was revealed. It could be when a Bedouin asked the Messenger ﷺ, "is our Lord near so we can have a secret conversation, or is he far away that we have to call out Lord?" This was revealed to explain the meaning of *"surely I am near."* Imam Razi ﷺ continues, by saying some ignorant people claim, "Du'a is something without benefits", and they argue:

1. If something will happen than it will happen anyway. If something is not to happen then it wouldn't happen; so then what is the need of Du'a? Allah ﷻ knows what man needs.
2. Allah ﷻ the Almighty is the Knower of all secrets so what is the need of Du'a? Again, He knows what man needs.
3. If the object of Du'a is the benefit of man then why does doesn't the "Most generous" give it without asking?
4. It is well-established fact from the texts and reason that the highest station of piety is being satisfied by the Divine will and Du'a negates this when one is requesting and preferring one's own wish, over Divine will.
5. Du'a is like making a command or prohibition; and that for man, with regards to his Lord, is blasphemous.
6. The Messenger ﷺ said Allah ﷻ says "Whoever is kept from asking me because of my zikr, I shall give him better than those who ask."

They say in light of these arguments it is better not make a Du'a. However, Imam Razi ﷺ strongly rejects this view and he says the overwhelming majority of scholars regard Du'a as a key form of worship.

He discusses the excellence of Du'a and says: "In Du'a there is no intermediary between man and the Lord it is a direct dialogue."

Secondly: the phrase *"when My servants ask about Me"*, points to "the servant is for Him" and this saying "I am near" indicates that the Lord is for the servant.

Thirdly, the verse does not say "Man is near Allah ﷻ", it says *"I am near."* So the nearness is from the Lord who is capable of being near though His Mercy and Grace.

Fourthly, the caller concentrates and fully focuses on his need passionately. With deep conviction he puts his trust in Allah ﷻ and calls him eventually. This proves that Du'a brings us closer to the Master, so Du'a is the best form of worship. The glorious Quran declares,

"Your Lord said call upon me and I will answer you" (Surah Ghafir[40], ayah 60)

In fact, Allah ﷻ is annoyed with those people who don't ask from Him.

"Then why did they not call upon us at the time of trouble, hardened and shaitaan decorated the deeds they used to do" (Surah An`am[6], ayah 43)

The Messenger ﷺ said, "When one of you says 'O Lord forgive me if you wish', he should stress and say 'O Lord, forgive me' and he said Du'a is the essence of worship and "Du'a is worship." Allah ﷻ tells us in the Quran:

"Say! What does my Lord care for you if you don't pray for him" (Surah al-Furqan[25], ayah 77)

The gist of his argument is that the purpose of Du'a is not merely giving information but it is an expression of the devotion, the humility and turning to Allah ﷻ whole heartedly. If this is the aim of Du'a then all those doubts raised by the ignorant people disappear. In response to the argument that Du'a is not answered, he cites the hadith where the Messenger ﷺ says, "a Du'a of a Muslim is never rejected outright as long as he doesn't ask for a forbidden thing or breaking of ties." Either his du'a will be fulfilled or recorded and saved for the hereafter or Allah ﷻ will divert away from him a calamity."

The intimate nature of Du'a is illustrated by the numerous examples of the Du'a that were made by the Prophets. For example, after the construction of the Ka'ba, Ibrahim عليه السلام turns to his Lord and prays,

"O Lord accept this from us, for you are all Listening and all Knowing." (Surah al-Baqara [2], ayah 127).

He continues to seek more and begs,

"O Lord! Send amongst them a Messenger who will recite your verses and teach them the book and wisdom." (Surah al-Baqara *[2], ayah 129)*

Allah ﷻ granted the Great Patriarch عليه السلام, his wish.

Du'a is a simple way of keeping in touch with Allah ﷻ. For almost every daily activity, a Prophetic Du'a can be found. From the time of waking up, to flying in the airplane; from eating a veggie burger to making business transactions.

These Du'a not only give barakah (spiritual blessing) to our mundane routines, but will make them easy. They will facilitate the difficult tasks and give the worldly and physical activities a spiritual dimension.

Du’a for the 15th of Sha’ban

Arabic

اَللّٰهُمَّ يَا ذَا الْمَنِّ وَلَا يُمَنُّ عَلَيْهِؕ يَا ذَا الْجَلَالِ وَالْاِكْرَامِؕ يَا ذَا
الطَّوْلِ وَالْاِنْعَامِؕ لَا اِلٰهَ اِلَّا اَنْتَ ظَهْرُ اللَّاجِيْنَؕ وَجَارُ
الْمُسْتَجِيْرِيْنَؕ وَاَمَانُ الْخَائِفِيْنَؕ اَللّٰهُمَّ اِنْ كُنْتَ كَتَبْتَنِيْ
عِنْدَكَ فِيْ اُمِّ الْكِتٰبِ شَقِيًّا اَوْ مَحْرُوْمًا اَوْ مَطْرُوْدًا اَوْ مُقَتَّرًا
عَلَيَّ فِي الرِّزْقِ فَامْحُ اللّٰهُمَّ بِفَضْلِكَ شَقَاوَتِيْ وَحِرْمَانِيْ وَطَرْدِيْ
وَاِقْتَارَ رِزْقِيْؕ وَاَثْبِتْنِيْ عِنْدَكَ فِيْ اُمِّ الْكِتٰبِ سَعِيْدًا مَّرْزُوْقًا
مُّوَفَّقًا لِّلْخَيْرَاتِؕ فَاِنَّكَ قُلْتَ وَقَوْلُكَ الْحَقُّ فِيْ كِتَابِكَ الْمُنَزَّلِ
عَلٰى لِسَانِ نَبِيِّكَ الْمُرْسَلِؕ يَمْحُوا اللّٰهُ مَا يَشَآءُ وَيُثْبِتُ وَعِنْدَهٗ
اُمُّ الْكِتٰبِ ۝ اِلٰهِيْ بِالتَّجَلِّي الْاَعْظَمِؕ فِيْ لَيْلَةِ النِّصْفِ مِنْ شَهْرِ
شَعْبَانَ الْمُكَرَّمِؕ الَّتِيْ يُفْرَقُ فِيْهَا كُلُّ اَمْرٍ حَكِيْمٍ وَّيُبْرَمُؕ
اَنْ تَكْشِفَ عَنَّا مِنَ الْبَلَاءِ وَالْبَلْوَآءِ مَا نَعْلَمُ وَمَا لَا نَعْلَمُؕ وَ
اَنْتَ بِهٖ اَعْلَمُؕ اِنَّكَ اَنْتَ الْاَعَزُّ الْاَكْرَمُؕ وَصَلَّى اللّٰهُ تَعَالٰى عَلٰى
سَيِّدِنَا مُحَمَّدٍ وَّعَلٰى اٰلِهٖ وَاَصْحَابِهٖ وَسَلَّمَ وَالْحَمْدُ لِلّٰهِ رَبِّ الْعٰلَمِيْنَ ۝

English translation

O Allah! You shower favours on everyone and no one can do You any favour. O the Possessor of Majesty and Honour, O The Distributor of bounty and rewards, there is no one worthy of worship except You. You help the fallen and provide refuge to the refugees and give peace to those who are in fear.

O Allah! If in the Mother of All Books that is with You, You have written me down as someone who is doubtful of achieving salvation, or deprived, or rejected or without enough sustenance,

Then, O Allah, with Your Grace remove all of these misfortunes from me and in the Mother of All Books that is with You, establish me as someone who is blessed, with abundant provision and charitable good deeds.

Indeed, what You said in The Book You sent through the tongue of Your Blessed Prophet is true.

That Allah changes and establishes what He wants and with Him is the Mother of All Books. O My Lord! For the sake of Your Divine Manifestation. On this fifteenth night of the blessed month of Sha'ban, in which You issue all Wise and Irrevocable Decrees, remove from us all calamities and hardships, those that we know about as well as those that we don't, while You know everything.

Truly, You are the Most Powerful, Most Generous. and may Allah the Exalted shower blessings and peace on Sayyidina Muhammad, and on his family and his companions. And all praise is for Allah, Lord of the worlds.

English transliteration

Allahumma Yaa Dhal Manni walaa yumannu ‘Alayh YaaDhal Jalaali wa’l Ikraam.

Yaa Dhat-Tawli wa’l In’aam Laa Ilaaha illa anta Zahru’llaajeen wa jaaru’l mustajeereen wa amaanu’l khaaifeen

Allahumma in kunta katabtanee ‘Indaka fee Ummil Kitabi Shaqiyyan aw mahruman aw matrudan aw muqattaran ‘alayya fi’rrizqi

Fa’mhuAllahumma biFadlika, Shaqaawatee wa hirmaanee wa tardee wa’qtitaara rizqee Wa-athbitnee ‘Indaka fee Ummil Kitabi

Sa’eedan marzuqan muwaffaqan li’lkhayraati Fa Innaka Qulta wa Qawluka’l Haqq Fee Kitabika’l munzal ‘alaa lisaani Nabiyyika’l Mursal

Yamhullahu maa Yashaa’u wa yuthbit Wa ‘Indahu Ummul Kitab Ilaahi Bittajalli’l A’zam, Fee laylatin-nisfi min shahri Sha’ban al-Mukarram Allatee yufraqu feehaa kullu amrin hakeemin wa yubram An takshifa ‘annaa mina’l ballaai wa’l balwaai.

Maa na’lamu wa maa laa na’lam Wa anta bihi a’lam. Innaka anta’l A’azzu’l Akram Wa Sallallahu Ta’ala ‘alaa Sayyidina Muhammad-in Wa ‘alaa aalihi wa as’haabihi wa sallam Wa’l Hamdu Lillahi Rabbi’l alameen.

Prayers of the Prophets & the Righteous

The Prophet Zakariyah ﵇ prays for righteous children:

﴿ هُنَالِكَ دَعَا زَكَرِيَّا رَبَّهُۥ ۖ قَالَ رَبِّ هَبْ لِى مِن لَّدُنكَ ذُرِّيَّةً طَيِّبَةً ۖ إِنَّكَ سَمِيعُ ٱلدُّعَآءِ ٣٨ ﴾

"Lord from your grace grants me virtuous offspring: you hear every prayer" (Surah al-i- Imran[3], ayah 38)

Zakariyah ﵇ was overwhelmed to see the variety of out-of-season fruits in Maryam's chamber so much so that despite knowing that his wife was infertile and he himself was an old man, he still longs for a child. So he humbly begs God for a righteous child. The Almighty, All-Hearing God grants him his prayer. The Prophet Jesus ﵇ prays for food:

﴿ قَالَ عِيسَى ٱبْنُ مَرْيَمَ ٱللَّهُمَّ رَبَّنَآ أَنزِلْ عَلَيْنَا مَآئِدَةً مِّنَ ٱلسَّمَآءِ تَكُونُ لَنَا عِيدًا لِّأَوَّلِنَا وَءَاخِرِنَا وَءَايَةً مِّنكَ ۖ وَٱرْزُقْنَا وَأَنتَ خَيْرُ ٱلرَّٰزِقِينَ ١١٤ ﴾

When the disciples of Jesus ﵇ asked him "can your lord send down a feast to us from heaven?" Jesus ﵇ prayed "Lord, send them to us a feast from heaven so that we can have a festival- the first and the last of us- and a sign from you. Provide for us, you are the best provider" (Surah al-Maidah[5], ayah 114)

The Prophet Shoaib عليه السلام prays for victory:

When the arrogant leaders of his community threatened to banish Shoaib عليه السلام and his followers, he turned to the lord in prayer:

﴿ ... رَبَّنَا ٱفْتَحْ بَيْنَنَا وَبَيْنَ قَوْمِنَا بِٱلْحَقِّ وَأَنتَ خَيْرُ ٱلْفَٰتِحِينَ ﴿٨٩﴾ ﴾

"Our Lord, let the truth be known and judge between us and our people, for you are the best judge." (Surah al-A'raf[7], ayah 89)

He عليه السلام also prayed,

﴿ ... إِنْ أُرِيدُ إِلَّا ٱلْإِصْلَٰحَ مَا ٱسْتَطَعْتُ ۚ وَمَا تَوْفِيقِىٓ إِلَّا بِٱللَّهِ ۚ عَلَيْهِ تَوَكَّلْتُ وَإِلَيْهِ أُنِيبُ ﴿٨٨﴾ ﴾

"I cannot succeed without God's help: I trust in him and always turn to him" (Surah Hud[11], ayah 88)

The Prophet Adam عليه السلام prays for forgiveness:

Once on the earth, Adam عليه السلام and Eve عليها السلام immediately realised their mistake and how the Satan had lured them into temptation, so they prayed:

﴿ قَالَا رَبَّنَا ظَلَمْنَآ أَنفُسَنَا وَإِن لَّمْ تَغْفِرْ لَنَا وَتَرْحَمْنَا لَنَكُونَنَّ مِنَ ٱلْخَٰسِرِينَ ﴿٢٣﴾ ﴾

"Our Lord, we have wrong our souls: if you do not forgive us and have mercy, we shall be lost." (Surah al-A'raf[7], ayah 23)

The prophet Yusuf عليه السلام prays for bliss in the afterlife:

﴿ ۞ رَبِّ قَدْ ءَاتَيْتَنِى مِنَ ٱلْمُلْكِ وَعَلَّمْتَنِى مِن تَأْوِيلِ ٱلْأَحَادِيثِ ۚ فَاطِرَ ٱلسَّمَٰوَٰتِ وَٱلْأَرْضِ
أَنتَ وَلِىِّۦ فِى ٱلدُّنْيَا وَٱلْءَاخِرَةِ ۖ تَوَفَّنِى مُسْلِمًا وَأَلْحِقْنِى بِٱلصَّٰلِحِينَ ﴿١٠١﴾ ﴾

"Creator of heavens and the earth, you are my protector in this world and in the hereafter. Let me die in true devotion to you. Join me with the righteous." (Surah Yusuf[12], ayah 101)

The prophet Yusuf ﵇ had gone through hard times: the jealousy and hostility of his brothers, separation from his family, temptations by Zulaikha, the trial and the disgrace of imprisonment. However, after that he lived a life of ease, luxury and affluence. As a man of God he understands the fleeting and the temporary nature of worldly success. He knew that material wealth is not the answer to human yearnings and everlasting that is after life. Imam Razi ﵀ comments at length on the transient and temporary nature of material wealth and says “sadly I have all these and I am fed up of them so I often recite this prayer of Yusuf”.

The prophet Ibrahim’s ﵇ prayer for the family:

This is a prayer that all Muslims say at the end of salah:

﴿ رَبَّنَا ٱغْفِرْ لِى وَلِوَٰلِدَىَّ وَلِلْمُؤْمِنِينَ يَوْمَ يَقُومُ ٱلْحِسَابُ ﴿٤١﴾ ﴾

“Lord, grant that I and my offspring may keep up the prayer. Our lord accepts my request. Our lord, forgive me, my parents and the believers on the day of reckoning” (Surah Ibrahim[14], ayah 41)

The prophet Yaqub ﵇ pours his sorrow before the Lord:

Yaqub ﵇ was old and frail but longed for his beloved son. Yusuf ﵇ so prayed,

﴿ قَالَ إِنَّمَآ أَشْكُوا۟ بَثِّى وَحُزْنِىٓ إِلَى ٱللَّهِ وَأَعْلَمُ مِنَ ٱللَّهِ مَا لَا تَعْلَمُونَ ﴿٨٦﴾ ﴾

“I plead my grief and sorrow before God”. (Surah Yusuf[12], ayah 86)

The prophet Musa’s ﵇ prayer for opening of the heart and the mind:

﴿ قَالَ رَبِّ ٱشْرَحْ لِى صَدْرِى ﴿٢٥﴾ وَيَسِّرْ لِىٓ أَمْرِى ﴿٢٦﴾ وَٱحْلُلْ عُقْدَةً مِّن لِّسَانِى ﴿٢٧﴾ يَفْقَهُوا۟ قَوْلِى ﴿٢٨﴾ ﴾

“Lord, lift up my heart and ease my task for me. Untie my tongue, so that they may understand my words”. (Surah Ta-ha[20], ayah 25-28)

When Musa ﵇ is commanded to go and preach to the Pharaoh, he is naturally daunted by his huge responsibility so asks God to help him.

Prophet Muhammad' ﷺ prayer for increase in knowledge:

﴿ ... قُل رَّبِّ زِدْنِي عِلْمًا ﴿١١٤﴾ ﴾

"O Lord, increase me in knowledge". (Surah Ta-ha[20], ayah 114)

The prophet Yunus ﷺ prays for forgiveness:

﴿ ... لَّآ إِلَٰهَ إِلَّآ أَنتَ سُبْحَٰنَكَ إِنِّي كُنتُ مِنَ ٱلظَّٰلِمِينَ ﴿٨٧﴾ ﴾

"There is no God but you, glory be to you,I was wrong." (Surah al-Anbiya[21],ayah 87)

This is a highly prized prayer at times of distress and anxiety.

The prophet Sulayman's ﷺ prayer:

After witnessing so many favours of the Lord Sulayman ﷺ prayed,

﴿ ... رَبِّ أَوْزِعْنِيٓ أَنْ أَشْكُرَ نِعْمَتَكَ ٱلَّتِيٓ أَنْعَمْتَ عَلَيَّ وَعَلَىٰ وَٰلِدَيَّ وَأَنْ أَعْمَلَ صَٰلِحًا تَرْضَىٰهُ وَأَدْخِلْنِي بِرَحْمَتِكَ فِي عِبَادِكَ ٱلصَّٰلِحِينَ ﴿١٩﴾ ﴾

"O Lord inspire me to be thankful for the blessings you have granted me and my parents and to do good deeds that please you. Admit me by your grace into the ranks of your righteous servants." (Surah an-Naml[27], ayah 19)

The Glorious Quran refers to several prayers of righteous people, here is a small selection of them:-

Prayer for the family:

﴿ ... رَبَّنَا هَبْ لَنَا مِنْ أَزْوَٰجِنَا وَذُرِّيَّٰتِنَا قُرَّةَ أَعْيُنٍ وَٱجْعَلْنَا لِلْمُتَّقِينَ إِمَامًا ﴿٧٤﴾ ﴾

"Our Lord gives us joy in our spouses and offspring. Make us good example to those who are God conscious people". (Surah al-Furqan[25], ayah 74)

For success in the world and the hereafter

﴿ ... رَبَّنَآ ءَاتِنَا فِي ٱلدُّنۡيَا حَسَنَةٗ وَفِي ٱلۡأٓخِرَةِ حَسَنَةٗ وَقِنَا عَذَابَ ٱلنَّارِ ٢٠١ ﴾

"Our Lord give us the best in the world and the best in the hereafter and protects us from the punishment of hell." (Surah al-Baqarah [2], ayah 210)

Prayer for patience:

﴿ ... رَبَّنَآ أَفۡرِغۡ عَلَيۡنَا صَبۡرٗا وَثَبِّتۡ أَقۡدَامَنَا وَٱنصُرۡنَا عَلَى ٱلۡقَوۡمِ ٱلۡكَٰفِرِينَ ٢٥٠ ﴾

"Our Lord, pour patience on us, makes us stand firm, and help us against the disbelievers".(Surah al-Baqarah [2], ayah 250)

This was the prayer of loyal warriors of Tahut which included when Prophet Daud عليه السلام. They were smaller in number standing against the mighty army of Goliath. However, Allah gave them victory.

Prayer for lightening burden, forgiveness and support:

This is a comprehensive prayer of the faithful:

﴿ ... رَبَّنَا لَا تُؤَاخِذۡنَآ إِن نَّسِينَآ أَوۡ أَخۡطَأۡنَاۚ رَبَّنَا وَلَا تَحۡمِلۡ عَلَيۡنَآ إِصۡرٗا كَمَا حَمَلۡتَهُۥ عَلَى
ٱلَّذِينَ مِن قَبۡلِنَاۚ رَبَّنَا وَلَا تُحَمِّلۡنَا مَا لَا طَاقَةَ لَنَا بِهِۦۖ وَٱعۡفُ عَنَّا وَٱغۡفِرۡ لَنَا وَٱرۡحَمۡنَآۚ
أَنتَ مَوۡلَىٰنَا فَٱنصُرۡنَا عَلَى ٱلۡقَوۡمِ ٱلۡكَٰفِرِينَ ٢٨٦ ﴾

"Lord does not take us to task if we forget or make mistakes. Lord, do not burden us as you burdened those before us. Lord do not burden us with more than we have strength to beer. Pardon us, forgive us, and have mercy on us. You are our protector, so help us against the disbelievers." (Surah al-Baqarah [2], ayah 286)

Seeking Lord's protection from the Satan:

﴿ وَقُل رَّبِّ أَعُوذُ بِكَ مِنۡ هَمَزَٰتِ ٱلشَّيَٰطِينِ ٩٧ وَأَعُوذُ بِكَ رَبِّ أَن يَحۡضُرُونِ ٩٨ ﴾

"Oh Lord I seek your protection from the goodings of the evil ones; I seek refuge with you Lord, so that they may not come near me." (Surah al-Muminun[23], ayah 97-98)

Seeking forgiveness for the dead:

This prayer we are told is the prayer of people of Madina in which they pray for the dead:

﴿... رَبَّنَا ٱغۡفِرۡ لَنَا وَلِإِخۡوَٰنِنَا ٱلَّذِينَ سَبَقُونَا بِٱلۡإِيمَٰنِ وَلَا تَجۡعَلۡ فِي قُلُوبِنَا غِلّٗا لِّلَّذِينَ ءَامَنُواْ رَبَّنَآ إِنَّكَ رَءُوفٞ رَّحِيمٌ ١٠﴾

"Lord forgives us our sins and the sins of our brothers who believed before us, and leave no malice in our hearts towards those who believe. Lord, you are truly compassionate and merciful." (Surah al-Hashr[50], ayah 10)

Learning to forgive

On the night of repentance we seek forgiveness from Allah, we repent. However, this would be incomplete and meaningless if we didn't learn to forgive others. Here we shall explore this wonderful virtue, what is forgiveness? How to forgive? What are the benefits of forgiveness?

Human beings are social creatures, living together as families in neighbourhoods, communities and towns. The infrastructure of roads, transport, institutions and facilities for leisure and recreation all are a testimony of hard work and a long torturous history. This economic prosperity is a result of many compromises where individuals and groups have willingly and unwillingly given and taken. People have been victims as well as perpetrators of injustice. However, people have learnt to forgive and move on. It is quality of being tolerant to others and the spirit of compassion that has been the source of this social cohesion and prosperity.

At the heart of all this is the virtue of forgiveness. **For Muslims forgiveness is Obligatory**. Forgiveness is a moral virtue that helps to build peace and reconciliation. Forgiveness is to forsake revenge when one is capable of exacting revenge. Michael Henderson an expert on forgiveness and peace maker defines forgiveness as "the willingness to cease to feel resentment against an offender. It is surrendering the right to get even." (Forgiveness, breaking the chain of hatred).

The Quran teaches that God is the Forgiving (al-Ghafir), the absolutely Forgiving (al-Ghaffar) and the most oft Forgiving (al-Ghafoor). Thus, the Quran provides us excellent examples and role models of forgiveness. We will also read how wonderfully forgiving the Messenger of Islam ﷺ was.

"Forgiveness allows us to let go of the pain in the memory and if we let go of the pain in the memory we can have the memory but it does not control us. When memory controls us we are the puppets of the past" (The Garden of Forgiveness in Beirut by A. Asseily).

Forgiveness is a powerful virtue for displacing hard feelings, it empowers the victim to release resentment, hatred, malice and thoughts of revenge. When you forgive, you dissociate yourself from the negative feelings that keep reminding yourself of the offence done against you. This diminishes the negative feelings against the other and gives you a sense of control and freedom that results in a happier life.

Research shows that forgiveness has health benefits too. Bitterness, hatred, grudges and desire for revenge is known to increase blood pressure and symptoms of stress. On the other hand forgiveness leads to improvement in health; this is a result of lower blood pressure, less hostility, less anxiety and depression. Forgiveness is a positive feeling, attitude and behaviour that naturally helps one better manage anger, build better relationships and win more friends. On the whole forgiveness is a complete remedy for moral and spiritual well-being.

Read the following beautiful stories of Forgiveness from the life of our Master and teacher Muhammad ﷺ . As we practice forgiveness we will become closer to him. This is our Islamic duty. Since forgiveness is a difficult task I have highlighted many examples from the Prophet's ﷺ life and forgiveness is challenging and hard work! The examples that follow illustrate beautifully how the Prophet ﷺ forgave even his bitterest enemies. Allah said to the Messenger ﷺ, *"Forgive, enjoin the good, and turn away from the ignorant." (Surah al-A'raf[7], ayah 199)*

The Prophet ﷺ asked Jibril عليه السلام to explain the meaning of forgiveness. He said "Allah tells you to befriend those who break off from you, give to those who refuse to give to you and overlook the faults of those who are unjust to you."

In the battle of Uhud, the Prophet's ﷺ tooth was broken and his face was badly cut. The Companions were extremely saddened and angry by this and appealed to the Prophet to curse the Makkans who had done this. He replied, "I was not sent to curse but sent as a summoner and a mercy. O Allah, guide my people for they do not know." (Haykal)

Rejected, humiliated and physically injured

One of the most moving incidents in the Prophet's ﷺ life was his trip to the town of Ta'if that was nearby Makkah. After he became disillusioned with the Makkans, the Prophet ﷺ thought about preaching his message in the people of Ta'if. However, it turned out to be an extremely humiliating experience. Not only did they refuse to listen to him, but they threw him out of town. They set upon him the street-urchins, vagabonds and children, who threw stones at him.

He ﷺwas badly injured, so much so that his sandals were filled with blood. He took refuge in an orchard outside the town. He looked up at the cloud and saw Jibril عليه السلام saying "Allah has heard what people said to you and how they rejected you. He has sent the angel of the mountains to you." The angel gave salutations of peace to the Prophet ﷺ and said, "I am at your service. If you wish, I will cause the two mountains of Akhshabayn to crush the people of Ta'if." The Prophet ﷺ replied, "I wish that Allah will bring forth from them generations who will worship Him alone and associate none with Him." (Bukhari)

When we analyse this prophetic forgiveness, we notice a process of forgiveness, firstly the prophet ﷺ explores his ﷺ pain and realises that it is of limited nature, he ﷺ recognises that he ﷺ has been unfairly insulted and punished. Secondly, he ﷺ is presented with the option of taking revenge but he ﷺ considers forgiveness. Next, the prophet ﷺ shows empathy and compassion for people of Taif. Finally, the mercy for the world ﷺ forgives and even prays for the perpetrators.

Forgiving the enemies

Similarly, the Prophet's ﷺ forgiveness of the Makkans after the victory of Makkah must be classed as one of the most remarkable examples of forgiveness in the annals of history. On that historic day, the Makkan public and leaders were all gathered in the Kabah, standing as prisoners anxiously waiting their fate. For nearly twenty years they had persecuted him, planned his assassination, murdered his uncle and many close friends. They feared that they would be all wiped out. The Prophet ﷺ stood up, after praising Allah, and asked them "what do you think I will do with you?" They replied as one, "You are a generous brother and generous nephew." The Prophet ﷺ smiled and said, "I say to you what my brother Yusuf said, 'There is no blame on you: go, you are all free.'" (Haykal)

Anas رضي الله عنه reports that "the next morning at dawn, eight Makkan men came with the intention of killing the Prophet ﷺ. They were seized. However, the Prophet ﷺ ordered that they should be freed. The Qur'anic verse was revealed to record this incident, *"He is the one who restrained their hands from you.' (Surah al-Fath[48], ayah 24)"* (Muslim)

There was a sinister magician by the name of Labid ibn al-Azam. He once performed magic on the Prophet ﷺ that had dire effects on his health. The spell was eventually broken after the revelation of Surah al-Falaq and Surah Al-Nas. Labid was exposed, but the Prophet ﷺ neither chided nor punished him. (Haykal)

Aisha رضي الله عنها succinctly sums up the Prophet's forgiving and clement nature: "I never saw the Messenger ﷺ ever take revenge for an injustice done to him, he never struck anyone with his hands except in the battlefield nor did he ever hit a servant or a woman." (Bukhari)

Dealing with an assassin

The Muslim army was returning from an expedition lead by the Prophet ﷺ. It was noon and the scorching sun forced them to stop and rest. Everyone found a place for themselves. The Prophet ﷺ also took a nap under a tree. An enemy soldier by the name of Ghawrith ibn Harris was watching and, taking advantage of this situation, took out his sword and approached the Prophet ﷺ stealthily. The Prophet ﷺ opened his eyes and saw the danger. Ghawrith said, "Who will save you from me?" Without any fear, the Prophet ﷺ replied with full faith, "My Lord will save me!" Upon hearing this, Ghawrith began to tremble and the sword fell from his hands. The Prophet ﷺ quickly picked up the sword and said, "Now tell me, who will save you from me?" He remorsefully said, "Become the one who is good to his captives." The Prophet ﷺ forgave him and let him go. (Bukhari)

Anas رضي الله عنه reported that, "One day I was walking with the Messenger ﷺ. He was wearing a Najarani cloak with a thick border. A Bedouin grabbed it and pulled it so forcefully that it left a mark on his neck. Then he said, 'O Muhammad! Tell them to give me money which you have', so he looked at him and smiled and ordered that he should be given something." (Bukhari)

Frequently Asked Questions

Q. Do we have to confess our sins in front of someone?

A sin is the disobedience of God, it is going against divine will, violating a commandment. Therefore, it is a violation of God's right and He is the only one who we need to apologise to. The confession of sin before others is not an Islamic practice. We are taught to turn sincerely to our lord, who will listen to us and forgive us.

Q. Why did the Messenger ﷺ repent? I thought he was sinless and protected from sins?

Indeed the Prophet ﷺ repented seventy times a day. One explanation is that He is a role model for us all, therefore He was teaching us to repent. Secondly, He was extremely humble and this was an expression of His humility.

Q. Are gatherings on 15th Sha'ban innovation, bidah?

Bidah is an innovation in religion; something new appended to religion. As such it can be good or bad, condoned or condemned, praiseworthy or blameworthy.

Imam Bukhari narrates that Umar ﵁ gathered people for Tarawih prayers and said this is a good innovation. Whilst commenting on this hadith Hafiz Ibn Hajar says: "Bidah is something which has no precedent and if its application contravenes a sunnah it is a condemnable bidah. If it conforms to Shariah then it is a good bidah otherwise it is permissible."

This is also the view of Imam Shafi who divides bidah into bidah mahmooda (good) and bidah mazmooma (bad). Similarly Imam Baihaqi has said in his book "Munaqib": "Bidah is of two kinds, one that contravenes the Quran and hadith and is also against the consensus, that is misguided bidah, but any innovation which is for the benefit of the Muslims and is not against the Shariah is acceptable."

Other scholars have divided bidah into five categories:

- ✓ **Wajib**: This is any innovation which is for the benefit or welfare of the Muslims like the invention of the science of grammar, syntax, logics, and the punctuation of the Quran, etc. These formative sciences were nonexistent in the time of the Prophet ﷺ, and today they are used for the proper understanding of Islam. Learning them is therefore wajib.
- ✓ **Mustahab**: The building of roads is mustahab since people benefit from them. Similarly the building of minarets for Adhan aids in spreading the call of prayer and it is therefore regarded as a mustahab bidah.
- ✓ **Mubah**: This third category of innovation is mubah or permissible. For example wearing good clothes, eating varied and refined foods. These are all permissible.
- ✓ **Makruh**: Anything that has an element of extravagance is makruh, or offensive in the sight of Shariah. Like unnecessary decoration of Masjids and copies of the Quran.
- ✓ **Haram**: An innovation is haram if it is against the sunnah and has no benefit for the Muslims.

In light of the above, gatherings on the night of 15th Sha'ban are permissible. I, fuqaha from Hijaz and jurists have stressed that praying nafl together in jamaat particularly if they are invited to it are makruh. However, others stress that as long as the people are not specifically gathered for praying nafl together it is permissible to pray even nafl jamaat.

The fact is that people do not gather on lailut-ul-bar'ah to pray nafl together, they gather to listen to: Quran, speeches and naat and to do zikr and to read the Quran, as it is easy to do this in a group then alone. Those people who feel confident that they could spend the whole night themselves steeped in worship can do so. But, experience tells us that it's better to worship, learn and repent together sometimes. In Hilya it is stated "Jama'ah is not performed in nafl prayers, however, if it happens occasionally then it is permissible and not makruh."

Q. Is it true that the blessed Messenger ﷺ fasted regularly in Sha'ban ?

Aisha ﵂ Said "the Messenger ﷺ used to fast the whole month of Ramadhan and after that most of all in Sha'ban than any other month." (Bukhari, Ch. fasting of Sha'ban). It is a preparation for the great month of Ramadhan.

About the Author

Dr Musharraf Hussain OBE is the director of the Karimia Institute in Nottingham, UK. A vibrant Islamic organisation dedicated to promoting moral, social and spiritual development through worship, education and recreation for today's society. Dr Musharraf is commited to reviving the message of Islam and he is involved in several national initiatives:

- Chairman of the Christian-Muslim Forum.
- Trustee for the National Centre for Citizenship.
- Chairman of the UK-Indonesian Islamic Advisory Group.
- A fellow of Staffordshire University.
- A trustee of Muslim Hands.

He is also the author of numerous books and articles on Islam:

1. **Aqaid an-Nasfi:** A translation of the orthodox creed written in the 11th century.
2. **The Perfect Prayer:** This is a manual with details of the most important rituals of prayer according to the Hanafi fiqh.

3. **The Blessings of Ramadan:** Describes the virtues, benefits and philosophy of fasting as well as fiqh issues.
4. **Pearls of Wisdom:** A collection of forty Ahadith on the means of personal development, love, marriage and parents.
5. **Time to Marry:** The purpose, how and when of this great institution are explored from Islamic as well as modern viewpoint.
6. **Journey to Allah:** Translation of manual by Hafiz Adbul Karim on self-purification spiritual development
7. **Shortening of Long Hopes:** A translation of Ahadith collection by Ibn Abi Dunya on detaching oneself from the love of the world.
8. **Hajj: Going Back to Your Roots:** Manual containing details of fiqh and how to perform hajj. With maps, diagrams and indispensable health guidelines.
9. **Dua & Salah made simple:** Prayers that everyone must know.
10. **Learning to read Quran:** An Arabic reader in 2 parts.
11. **Beliefs and Religions: Islam**. Published by Thornes Nelson. An Introduction to Islamic teachings for British secondary schools.
12. **Seven Steps to Moral Living.** Published by Kube Publisher. A guide for character building and developing self-discipline.
13. **Selected Questions & Answers from Fatawa Rizwiyya**. A collection of more than a hundred Question & Answers on the subject of cleanliness.
14. The "People and Places Series" is a series of booklets available free of charge from the Invitation Publications
15. **The Tragedy of Karbala:** Outlines the brief history of the battle of Karbala and its consequences. A tribute to the Prophet's ﷺ family.
16. **Celebrations of the Prophet's ﷺ Birthday:** Polemical discussion of the virtues of celebrating the birth of the Greatest Prophet of God.
17. **Maulana Ahmed Raza Khan ﷺ:** Introduction to the life works of one of the greatest scholars of the twentieth century.
18. **Isra' & Mi'raj: The Prophet's ﷺ Glorious Night Journey and Ascent to Heaven:** This booklet describes this wonderful miracle in the light of the glorious Quran and ahadith.

Many articles are available on our website, www.karimia.com, such as

1. British Muslims.
2. Caught in the consumer trap.
3. Friendship with a Grizzly.
4. Growing in Real strength.
5. The healthy, wealthy and unhappy.
6. Ramadan: An antidote to Consumerism.
7. Ramadan: Month of Mercy.
8. Ramadan: time for reflection.
9. Jihad in Quran and Sunnah.
10. Women attending the Masjid.

The blessed Messenger ﷺ said, "the superiority of men of knowledge over others is like my superiority over one of you."
